The Essential

NELSON MANDELA

compiled by Robin Malan

DAVID PHILIP PUBLISHERS
Cape Town

MAYIBUYE BOOKS
University of the Western Cape, Bellville

First published 1997 in southern Africa by David Philip
Publishers (Pty) Ltd, 208 Werdmuller Centre, Claremont
7700 and Mayibuye Books, University of the Western
Cape, Private Bag X17, Bellville 7535

ISBN 0-86486-344-6

Mayibuye History and Literature Series No. 81

Printed in South Africa by National Book Printers,
Drukkery Street, Goodwood, Western Cape

CONTENTS

STUDENT

| 1918–34 | Childhood | 7 |
| 1934–41 | Becoming a Man | 8 |

LAWYER

| 1941–53 | A Man of the City | 9 |

POLITICIAN

Sept. 1953	No Easy Walk to Freedom	11
1955	Two Clear, Sunny Days	13
June 1956	During Our Lifetime	13
1956–60	Strength for the Struggles Ahead	15
March–Oct. 1960	We Are Not Anti-white	15
1961	A Life Neither of Us Wanted	17
May 1961	Time for You to Speak Out	17
June 1961	The Struggle Is My Life	19
1961--2	David Motsamayi Under Arrest	20
Oct. – Nov. 1962	Black Man in a White Court	21

PRISONER

20 April 1964	I Am Prepared to Die	27
15 April 1976	How Can My Spirits Ever Be Down?	30
1978 30	Going to the Movies	30
15 Oct. 1978	Upright Like a Field Marshal	31
2 Sept.	My Last Sin on Earth	33
1978 and 1984	Contact	34
June 1980	After 16 June 1976	34
March 1981	The Prisoner and the Princess	36

Feb. 1985	Your Love and Support	37
Feb. 1985	Prisoners Cannot Enter into Contracts	38
Feb. 1986	The Prisoner's New Clothes	39
Dec. 1986	Taken for a Ride	40
Dec. 1988	Against Doctor's Orders	41
July 1989	Tied up in Knots	41
July 1989	No Self-respecting Freedom Fighter	42
Dec. 1989	An Honest Commitment to Peace	44

STATESMAN

Feb. 1990	Meeting the People	47
Feb. 1990	I Stand Here Before You	47
Feb. 1990	Return to School and Learn	49
Feb. 1990	End This War Now!	50
Nov. 1990	We Salute the Mothers	52
Dec. 1991	Like a Schoolmaster	53
Dec. 1991	Less Than Frank	54
April 1992	The Pain I Have Gone Through	56
June 1992	The Last Straw	57
June 1992	We Keep Talking Peace	58
April 1993	To Cofimvaba, to Pay My Respects	59
April 1993	Honour This Soldier for Peace	60
April 1993	A Life-long Conversation	61
June 1993	A Job to Do	62
May 1994	What the Doctor Ordered	63
May 1994	Free at Last	63

PRESIDENT

May 1994	The Day Dawned	65
May 1994	I Do Hereby Swear	65
May 1994	Never, Never and Never Again	66
May 1994	That Other Force	69
1994	Discovering the Secret	72
April 1997	A Very Amazing Experience	72
	Sources	74

STUDENT

1918–34   Childhood
Autobiography

My father bestowed upon me at birth the name Rolihlahla. In Xhosa, Rolihlahla literally means 'pulling the branch of a tree', but its colloquial meaning more accurately would be 'troublemaker'. I do not believe that names are destiny or that my father somehow divined my future, but in later years, friends and relatives would ascribe to my birth name the many storms I have both caused and weathered.

After a brief period of mourning, my mother informed me that I would be leaving Qunu. I did not ask her why, or where I was going. I mourned less for my father than for the world I was leaving behind. Qunu was all that I knew, and I loved it in the unconditional way that a child loves his first home. I turned and looked at my village. I imagined my friends out hunting for small birds, drinking the sweet milk from the cow's udder, cavorting in the pond at the end of the stream. I could not imagine that the future I was walking towards could compare in any way with the past that I was leaving behind.

1934–41   Becoming a Man
Autobiography

Circumcision is a trial of bravery and stoicism; no anaesthetic is used; a man must suffer in silence. I was distressed that I had been disabled, however briefly, by the pain, and I did my best to hide my agony. A boy may cry; a man conceals his pain.

At the University College of Fort Hare I also joined the drama society and acted in a play about Abraham Lincoln. I played John Wilkes Booth, Lincoln's assassin.

On our return from Fort Hare, to escape these unwished for and unsuitable marriages Justice and I decided that the only choice remaining was to run away, and the only place to run to was Johannesburg.

LAWYER

1941–53   A Man of the City
Autobiography

At Wits, I met many people who were to share with me the ups and downs of the liberation struggle. During my first term I met Joe Slovo and his future wife, Ruth First. I began lifelong friendships with George Bizos and Bram Fischer, and with Ismail Meer.

Walter's house in Orlando was a mecca for activists and ANC members, and it was my home from home. The house was always full, and it seemed there was a perpetual discussion going on about politics. Albertina was a wise and wonderful presence.

My first son, Madiba Thembekile, was given my clan name of Madiba, but was known by the nickname Thembi. I had now produced an heir and perpetuated the Mandela name and the Madiba clan, which is one of the basic responsibilities of a Xhosa male.

The Defiance Campaign freed me from any lingering sense of doubt or inferiority I might still have felt. Now the white man had felt the power of my punches and I could walk upright like a man, and look everyone in the eye with the dignity that comes from not having succumbed to oppression and fear. I had come of age as a freedom fighter.

'Mandela and Tambo' read the brass plate on our office door. I had become a man of the city. I wore smart suits, I drove a colossal Oldsmobile, I commuted daily to a down-town office. I was thirty-five. My commitment to the struggle had become my life.

POLITICIAN

21 September 1953   No Easy Walk to Freedom
Presidential address to Annual Transvaal ANC Conference.
Nelson Mandela was banned and so forbidden to attend; the
speech was read on his behalf.

Since 1912 and year after year thereafter, in their homes, in
provincial and national gatherings, on trains and buses, in
the factories and on the farms, in cities, villages, shanty-
towns, schools and prisons, the African people have discussed the shameful misdeeds of those who rule the country.

Year after year they have raised their voices to condemn
the grinding poverty of the people, the low wages, the acute
shortage of land, the inhuman exploitation, and the whole
policy of white domination. But instead of more freedom,
repression began to grow in volume and intensity and it
seemed that all their sacrifices would end in smoke and
dust.

Today the whole country knows that their labours were
not in vain, for a new spirit and new ideas have gripped our
people. Today the people speak the language of action:
there is a mighty awakening among the men and women of
our country.

The day of reckoning between the forces of freedom and
those of reaction is not far off. I have not the slightest doubt
that when that day comes truth and justice will prevail.

From now on the activity of the Congressites must not be confined to speeches and resolutions. Their activities must find expression in wide-scale work among the masses, work which will enable them to make the greatest possible contact with the working people. You must defend and protect your trade unions. If you are not allowed to have your meetings publicly, then you must hold them over your machines in the factories, on the trains and buses as you travel home. You must have them in your villages and shanty-towns. You must make every home and every shack and every mud structure where our people live a branch of the trade union movement, and you must never surrender.

You must defend the right of African parents to decide the kind of education that shall be given to their children. Teach the children that the Africans are not one iota inferior to Europeans. Establish your own community schools where the right kind of education will be given to our children. If it becomes dangerous or impossible to have these schools, then again you must make every home, every shack or rickety structure a centre of learning for our children. Never surrender to the inhuman and barbaric theories of Verwoerd.

You can see that there is no easy walk to freedom anywhere and many of us will have to pass through the valley of the shadow of death again and again before we reach the mountain-tops of our desires. Dangers and difficulties have not deterred us in the past; they will not frighten us now. But we must be prepared for them like men who mean business and who do not waste energy in vain talk and idle action. The way of preparation of action lies in our making our organisation the bright and shining instrument that will cleave its way to Africa's freedom.

[The final paragraph, including the phrase 'no easy walk to freedom', was adapted from a speech by Nehru.]

1955   Two Clear, Sunny Days
Autobiography

On those two clear, sunny days I drove to the Congress of the People in Kliptown with Walter. We were both under banning orders, so we found a place at the edge of the crowd where we could observe without mixing in or being seen. When the police raid began, while my instinct was to stay and help, discretion seemed the wiser course, and I returned to Johannesburg.

June 1956   During Our Lifetime
Article

The adoption of the Freedom Charter by the Congress of the People was widely recognised both at home and abroad as an event of major political significance in the life of this country.

Never before has any document or conference been so widely acclaimed and discussed by the democratic movement in South Africa. Never before has any document or conference constituted such a serious and formidable challenge to the racial and anti-popular policies of the country.

For the first time in the history of our country the democratic forces, irrespective of race, ideological conviction, party affiliation or religious belief, have renounced and discarded racialism in all its ramifications, clearly defined their aims and objects, and united in a common programme of action.

The Charter is more than a mere list of demands for democratic reforms. It is a revolutionary document precisely because the changes it envisages cannot be won without breaking up the economic and political set-up of present South Africa.

While the Charter proclaims democratic changes of a far-reaching nature, it is by no means a blueprint for a socialist state but a programme for the unification of various classes and groupings among the people on a democratic basis. Under socialism the workers hold state power. They and the peasants own the means of production, the land, the factories, and the mills. The Charter does not contemplate such profound economic and political changes. Its declaration 'The People Shall Govern!' visualises the transfer of power not to any single social class but to all the people of this country, be they workers, peasants, professional men, or petty-bourgeoisie.

The democratic struggle in South Africa is conducted by an alliance of various classes and political groupings among the non-European people, supported by white democrats. African, Coloured, and Indian workers and peasants, traders and merchants, students and teachers, doctors and lawyers, and various other classes and groupings; all participate in the struggle against racial inequality and for full democratic rights.

The Congress movement is rapidly becoming the real voice of South Africa. If this united front is strengthened and developed the Freedom Charter will be transformed into a dynamic and living instrument and we shall vanquish all opposition and win the South Africa of our dreams during our lifetime.

1956–60 *Strength for the Struggles Ahead*
Autobiography

'Mandela, we have a warrant for your arrest. Come with me.' I looked at the warrant, and the words leapt out at me: 'HOOGVERRAAD – HIGH TREASON'.

One afternoon, during a recess in the preparatory examination, I noticed a lovely young woman waiting for the bus. The moment I first glimpsed Winnie Nomzamo, I knew that I wanted to have her as my wife.

March–October 1960 *We Are Not Anti-white*
Testimony in the Treason Trial

DEFENCE: Do you think that, apart from the increase in your membership, the 1952 Defiance Campaign had any other result?

MANDELA: Yes, most certainly. Firstly, it pricked the conscience of the European public, which became aware in a

15

much more clear manner of the sufferings and disabilities of the African people. It led directly to the formation of the Congress of Democrats. It also influenced the formation of the Liberal Party. It also led to discussions on the policies of apartheid at the United Nations, and I think to that extent it was an outstanding success.

DEFENCE: Do you think it had any effect at all on the Government?

MANDELA: I think it had. After the Defiance Campaign the Government began talking about self-government for Africans, Bantustans. I do not believe, of course, that the Government was in any way sincere in saying it was part of Government policy to extend autonomy to Africans. I think they acted in order to deceive, but in spite of that deception one thing comes out very clearly and that is that they acknowledged the power of the Defiance Campaign, they felt that the striking power of the ANC had tremendously increased.

BENCH: Well, as a matter of fact, isn't your freedom a direct threat to the Europeans?

MANDELA: No, it is not a direct threat to the Europeans. We are not anti-white, we are against white supremacy and in struggling against white supremacy we have the support of some sections of the European population, and we have made this clear from time to time. As a matter of fact, in the letter we wrote to the then Prime Minister of the country, Dr Malan, before we launched the Defiance Campaign, we said that the campaign we were about to launch was not directed against any racial group. It was a campaign which was directed against laws which we considered unjust, and, time without number, the ANC has explained this. It is quite clear that the Congress has consistently preached a policy of race harmony, and we have condemned racialism no matter by whom it is professed.

1961   A Life Neither of Us Wanted
Autobiography

It was as though Winnie could read my thoughts. She knew I was about to embark on a life that neither of us wanted. If we were not convicted, I would go underground.

23 May 1961   Time for You to Speak Out
Letter to Sir De Villiers Graaff, leader of the white opposition United Party
Sir,

In one week's time, the Verwoerd Government intends to inaugurate its Republic. It is unnecessary to state that this intention has never been endorsed by the non-white majority of this country. The decision has been taken by little over half of the white community; it is opposed by every articulate group among the African, Coloured and Indian communities, who constitute the majority of this country.

The Government's intention to proceed, under these circumstances, has created conditions bordering on crisis. We have been excluded from the Commonwealth, and condemned 95 to 1 at the United Nations. Our trade is being boycotted, and foreign capital is being withdrawn. The country is becoming an armed camp, the Government preparing for civil war with increasingly heavy police and military apparatus, the non-white population for a general strike and long-term non-co-operation with the Government.

None of us can draw any satisfaction from this developing crisis. We, on our part, in the name of the African people – the majority of South Africans – have put forward serious proposals for a way out of the crisis. We have called on the Government to convene an elected National Convention of representatives of all races without delay, and to charge that Convention with the task of drawing up a new Constitution for this country which would be acceptable to all racial groups.

We can see no workable alternative to this proposal, except that the Nationalist Government proceeds to enforce a minority decision on all of us, with the certain consequence of still deeper crisis, and a continuing period of strife and disaster ahead. Stated bluntly, the alternatives appear to be these: talk it out, or shoot it out. Outside of the Nationalist Party, most of the important and influential bodies of public opinion have clearly decided to talk it out.

But where, Sir, does the United Party stand? We have yet to hear from this most important organisation. Or from you, its leader. If the country's leading statesmen fail to lead at this moment, then the worst is inevitable. It is time for you, Sir, and your party, to speak out. Are you for a democratic and peaceable solution to our problems? Are you, therefore, for a National Convention? We in South Africa, and the world outside, expect an answer. Silence at this time enables Dr Verwoerd to lead us onwards towards the brink of disaster.

We urge you strongly to speak out now. It is ten days to 31 May.

Yours faithfully,

Nelson Mandela

All-In African National Action Council

26 June 1961   The Struggle Is My Life

Press Release issued by Nelson Mandela from underground inside South Africa and published by the ANC in London

No power on earth can stop an oppressed people, determined to win their freedom.

Today is 26 June, a day known throughout the length and breadth of our country as Freedom Day. It is fit and proper that on this historic day I should speak to you and announce fresh plans for the opening of the second phase in the fight against the Verwoerd republic, and for a National Convention.

I am informed that a warrant for my arrest has been issued, and that the police are looking for me. The National Action Council has given full and serious consideration to this question, and has sought the advice of many trusted friends and bodies and they have advised me not to surrender myself. I have accepted this advice, and will not give myself up to a Government I do not recognise. Any serious politician will realise that under present-day conditions in this country, to seek for cheap martyrdom by handing myself to the police is naïve and criminal. We have an important programme before us and it is important to carry it out very seriously and without delay.

I have chosen this latter course, which is more difficult and which entails more risk and hardship than sitting in gaol. I have had to separate myself from my dear wife and children, from my mother and sisters, to live as an outlaw in my own land. I have had to close my business, to abandon my profession, and live in poverty and misery, as many of my people are doing. I will continue to act as the spokesman of the National Action Council during the phase that is unfolding and in the tough struggles that lie ahead. I shall fight the Government side by side with you, inch by inch, mile by mile, until victory is won. What are you going to do? Will you come along with us, or are you going to co-operate with the Government in its efforts to suppress the claims and aspirations of your own people? Or are you going to remain silent and neutral in a matter of life and death to my people, to our people? For my own part I have made my choice. I will not leave South Africa, nor will I surrender. Only through hardship, sacrifice and militant action can freedom be won. The struggle is my life. I will continue fighting for freedom until the end of my days.

1961–2 *David Motsamayi Under Arrest*
Autobiography

I knew in that instant that my life on the run was over; my seventeen months of 'freedom' as the 'Black Pimpernel' were about to end. Sergeant Vorster asked me to identify myself. I told him my name was David Motsamayi. He nodded, and then he said, 'Ag, you're Nelson Mandela, and you are under arrest!'

15 October–7 November 1962   Black Man in a White Court

Extracts from the court record. Nelson Mandela was charged with inciting people to strike illegally and with leaving the country without a valid passport.

MANDELA: Your Worship, I have elected to conduct my own defence. Some time during the progress of these proceedings, I hope to be able to indicate that this case is a trial of the aspirations of the African people, and because of that I thought it proper to conduct my own defence.

I want to apply for Your Worship's recusal from this case. I challenge the right of this Court to hear my case on two grounds.

Firstly, I challenge it because I fear that I will not be given a fair and proper trial. Secondly, I consider myself neither legally nor morally bound to obey laws made by a Parliament in which I have no representation.

In a political trial such as this one, which involves a clash of the aspirations of the African people and those of whites, the country's courts, as presently constituted, cannot be impartial and fair.

In such cases, whites are interested parties. To have a white judicial officer presiding, however high his esteem, and however strong his sense of fairness and justice, is to make whites judges in their own case.

The white man makes all the laws, he drags us before his courts and accuses us, and he sits in judgement over us.

It is fit and proper to raise the question sharply, what is this rigid colour-bar in the administration of justice? Why is it that in this courtroom I face a white magistrate, confronted by a white prosecutor, and escorted into the dock by a white orderly? Can anyone honestly and seriously suggest that in this type of atmosphere the scales of justice are evenly balanced?

I feel oppressed by the atmosphere of white domination that lurks all around in this courtroom. Somehow this atmosphere calls to mind the inhuman injustices caused to my people outside this courtroom by this same white domination.

It makes me feel that I am a black man in a white court. This should not be. I should feel perfectly at ease and at home with the assurance that I am being tried by a fellow South African who does not regard me as an inferior, entitled to a special type of justice.

I have the hope and confidence that Your Worship will not hear this objection lightly nor regard it as frivolous. I have decided to speak frankly and honestly because the injustice I have referred to contains the seeds of an extremely dangerous situation for our country and people. I make no threat when I say that unless these wrongs are remedied without delay, we might well find that even plain talk before the country's courts is too timid a method to draw the attention of the country to our political demands.

[The application for the recusal of the magistrate was refused.]

[After the Prosecutor's address to the Court, the Magistrate asked if the accused had anything to say]

MANDELA: Your Worship, I submit that I am guilty of no crime.

MAGISTRATE: Is that all you have to say?

MANDELA: Your Worship, with respect, if I had something more to say, I would have said it.

Nelson Mandela's address to the Court before sentence

MANDELA: The Court has found that I am guilty of incitement to commit an offence against the law which established a Republic in the Union of South Africa, as well as of leaving the country without a passport. But in weighing up the decision as to the sentence which is to be imposed for such an offence, the Court must take into account the question of responsibility, whether it is I who am responsible or whether, in fact, a large measure of the responsibility does not lie on the shoulders of the Government which promulgated that law, knowing that my people, who constitute the majority of the population of this country, were opposed to that law, and knowing further that every legal means of demonstrating that opposition had been closed to them by prior legislation, and by Government administrative action.

It has not been easy for me during the past period to take up the life of a man hunted continuously by the police, living separated from those who are closest to me, in my own country, facing continually the hazards of detection and of arrest. This has been a life infinitely more difficult than serving a prison sentence. No man in his right senses would voluntarily choose such a life in preference to the one of normal, family, social life which exists in every civilised country.

But there comes a time, as it came in my life, when a man is denied the right to live a normal life, when he can only live the life of an outlaw because the Government has so decreed to use the law to impose a state of outlawry upon him. I was driven to this situation, and I do not regret having taken the decisions that I did take. Other people will be driven in the same way in this country, by this very same force of police persecution and of administrative action by the Government, to follow my course, of that I am certain.

I do not believe, Your Worship, that this Court in inflicting penalties on me for the crimes for which I am convicted should be moved by the belief that penalties deter men from the course that they believe is right. History shows that penalties do not deter men when their conscience is aroused, nor will they deter my people or the colleagues with whom I have worked before.

For to men, freedom in their own land is the pinnacle of their ambitions, from which nothing can turn men of conviction aside. More powerful than my fear of the dreadful conditions to which I might be subjected is my hatred for the dreadful conditions to which my people are subjected outside prison throughout this country.

I hate the practice of race discrimination, and in my

hatred I am sustained by the fact that the overwhelming majority of mankind hate it equally. I hate the systematic inculcation of children with colour prejudice and I am sustained in that hatred by the fact that the overwhelming majority of mankind, here and abroad, are with me in that. I hate the racial arrogance which decrees that the good things in life shall be retained as the exclusive right of a minority of the population, and which reduces the majority of the population to a position of subservience and inferiority, and maintains them as voteless chattels to work where they are told and behave as they are told by the ruling minority. I am sustained in that hatred by the fact that the overwhelming majority of mankind both in this country and abroad are with me.

Nothing that this Court can do to me will change in any way that hatred in me, which can only be removed by the removal of the injustice and the inhumanity which I have sought to remove from the political, social, and economic life of this country. .

Whatever sentence Your Worship sees fit to impose upon me for the crime for which I have been convicted before this Court, may it rest assured that, when my sentence has been completed, I will still be moved, as men are always moved, by their consciences; I will still be moved by my dislike of the race discrimination against my people when I come out from serving my sentence, to take up again, as best I can, the struggle for the removal of those injustices until they are finally abolished once and for all.

I have done my duty to the people and to South Africa.

I have no doubt that posterity will pronounce that I was innocent and that the criminals that should have been brought before this Court are the members of the Verwoerd Government.

PRISONER

20 April 1964   I Am Prepared to Die
Statement from the dock at the start of the defence case in the Rivonia trial.

I am the first accused.

I hold a Bachelor's Degree in Arts and practised as an attorney in Johannesburg for a number of years in partnership with Oliver Tambo. I am a convicted prisoner serving five years for leaving the country without a permit and for inciting people to go on strike at the end of May 1961.

At the outset, I want to say that the suggestion made by the State in its opening that the struggle in South Africa is under the influence of foreigners or communists is wholly incorrect. I have done whatever I did, both as an individual and as a leader of my people, because of my experience in South Africa and my own proudly felt African background, and not because of what any outsider might have said.

In my youth in the Transkei I listened to the elders of my tribe telling stories of the old days. Among the tales they related to me were those of wars fought in defence of the fatherland. The names of Dingane and Bambata, Hintsa and Makana, Squngthi and Dalasile, Moshoeshoe and Sekhukuni, were praised as the glory of the entire African nation. I hoped then that life might offer me the opportunity to serve my people and make my own humble contribution to their freedom struggle. This is what has motivated me in all that I have done in relation to the charges made against me in this case.

I admit immediately that I was one of the persons who helped to form Umkhonto weSizwe, and that I played a prominent role in its affairs until I was arrested in August 1962.

I and the others who started the organisation did so because we believed that, as a result of Government policy, violence by the African people had become inevitable. All lawful modes of expressing opposition to this principle had been closed by legislation, and we were placed in a position in which we had either to accept a permanent state of inferiority, or to defy the Government. We chose to defy the law. We first broke the law in a way which avoided any recourse to violence; when this form was legislated against, and then the Government resorted to a show of force to crush opposition to its policies, only then did we decide to answer violence with violence.

This conclusion was not easily arrived at. The Government left us with no other choice. In the Manifesto of Umkhonto published on 16 December 1961 we said: 'The time comes in the life of any nation when there remain only two choices – submit or fight. That time has now come to South Africa. We shall not submit and we have no choice but to hit back by all means in our power in defence of our people, our future, and our freedom.'

This was our feeling in June of 1961. I can only say that I felt morally obliged to do what I did.

Our fight is against real, and not imaginary, hardships or,

to use the lanquage of the State Prosecutor, 'so-called hard-ships'. Basically, we fight against two features which are the hallmarks of African life in South Africa and which are entrenched by legislation which we seek to have repealed. These features are poverty and lack of human dignity, and we do not need communists or so-called 'agitators' to teach us about these things.

Above all, we want equal political rights, because without them our disabilities will be permanent. I know this sounds revolutionary to the whites in this country, because the majority of voters will be Africans. This makes the white man fear democracy.

But this fear cannot be allowed to stand in the way of the only solution which will guarantee racial harmony and freedom for all. It is not true that the enfranchisement of all will result in racial domination. Political division, based on colour, is entirely artificial and, when it disappears, so will the domination of one colour group by another. The ANC has spent half a century fighting against racialism. When it triumphs, it will not change that policy.

This then is what the ANC is fighting. Their struggle is a truly national one. It is a struggle of the African people, inspired by their own suffering and their own experience. It is a struggle for the right to live.

During my lifetime I have dedicated myself to this struggle of the African people. I have fought against white domination, and I have fought against black domination. I have cherished the ideal of a democratic and free society in which all persons live together in harmony and with equal opportunities. It is an ideal which I hope to live for and to achieve. But if needs be, it is an ideal for which I am prepared to die.

15 April 1976   How Can My Spirits Ever Be Down?
Letter to Winnie Madikizela Mandela

As I woke up on the morning of 25 February I was missing you and the children a great deal as always. Sometimes it's a wonderful experience to think back about precious moments spent with you, darling. I wonder what it'll be like when I return.

Your beautiful photo still stands about two feet above my left shoulder as I write this note. I dust it carefully every morning, for to do so gives me the pleasant feeling that I'm caressing you as in the old days. I start with that of Zeni, which is on the outer side, then Zindzi's and lastly yours, my darling Mum. I even touch your nose with mine to recapture the electric current that used to flush through my blood whenever I did so. How can my spirits ever be down when I enjoy the attention of so wonderful a lady?

I love you! Devotedly, Dalibunga

1978   Going to the Movies
Autobiography

We now had our own cinema. Almost every week we watched films on a sheet in a large room adjacent to our corridor. I recall one of the first ones was *The Mark of Zorro*,

with the swashbuckling Douglas Fairbanks, a movie that
was made in 1920. Later, we were permitted to select doc-
umentaries – a form that I preferred – and I began to skip
the conventional films. (Although I would never miss a
movie with Sophia Loren in it.)

15 October 1978   *Upright Like a Field Marshal*
Letter to Helen Joseph, old friend and veteran activist, the first
person to be placed under house arrest, for nine years, 1962–71.

Our dearest Helen,

Yes, I got your terrific letter. How you can inspire others!
Your congratulations and good wishes had a tremendous
effect on me. They wrenched me off this island, out of my
cell and put me right in the centre of the Golden City, in
Soweto, in Gould and Pritchard, on the road to Pretoria and
back, and into the lovely cottage at 35 Fanny Avenue.

My mind carries a picture that never fades in spite of the
years that have passed since I last saw you. You were standing in front of the house, like one waiting for the chickens
to come home to roost. Zami and Co were outside the gate
talking lively to one another. At that time I was travelling,
worried that I had left behind Zami all alone. Strange as that
may sound in the circumstances, the fact that you were still
there comforted me. I was confident that you would always
play the role of guardian angel to her. Perhaps that is one of
the reasons why the picture is unforgettable. But not even
in my wildest dream did I ever suspect that I would again
hear from you. Least of all, that I would have the opportu-

... ...luding your picture in the family album. Of ... ...ami and the children often speak of you. In her ... ...tter she mentioned Zazi's christening ceremony and ... special flight to Bloemfontein for the great occasion. ...e real surprise was yours which came two weeks later, followed by several photos from Muzi.

I immediately spotted a tall lady who stood upright like a field marshal. From her defiant and graceful pose, she seemed to enjoy carrying her seventy-three years. It is fitting that you should be godmother to Zazi and for Dr Moroka to be godfather – that is a tremendous combination. I sincerely hope that when Zazi grows up, that combination will be one of the driving forces in her life.

I am sorry that Zindzi has to live so far from you. My wish has always been that she should be near you, so that you can help Zami in guiding her. This is especially the case at her present age and with her ambitions. She and Zeni were too young when we parted and Zami's kind of life has brought a lot of emotional suffering on them. I always encourage them to come over to you whenever they can. It must have been a terrible blow to you to lose the old cat. I know how you loved it and how it was attached to you. I hope Lolita is equally attached and gives you the same pleasure as the old one. German shepherds are considered intelligent and reliable animals. I trust that Kwacha represents her breed well. That you have some company in the house is a source of comfort to me.

Finally, Helen, I should like to take this opportunity to thank you and all those who look after Zami and the children in my absence. The heat of the summer and the winter colds would have been difficult to bear without you all. I am keeping my right hand clean and warm because it has an important duty to perform, i.e. to hold yours very firmly. Meantime, your message of congratulations and good wishes has cut down my age by half. I feel and move like a lightweight in spite of the 76 kg I carry.

2 September 1979   My Last Sin on Earth
Letter to Winnie Madikizela Mandela

On 16 August I saw an orthopaedic surgeon and he examined my right heel which worries me now and again. That morning that the *Dias* carried me to Cape Town the sea was rough. The boat rocked on endlessly, taking every wave on its prows. Midway between the island and Cape Town an army of demons seemed to be on the rampage and the *Dias* was tossed about. I kept my eyes glued on a lifebelt a few paces away. There were about five officials between me and the belt, two young enough to be my grandsons. I said to myself, 'If something happens and this boat goes under, I will commit my last sin on earth and tender my humble apologies when I reach heaven. I will run over them all and be the first on that belt.' Fortunately no disaster overtook us.

1978 and 1984   Contact
Autobiography

When Zeni saw me, she practically tossed her tiny daughter to her husband and ran across the room to embrace me. I had not held my now grown-up daughter since she was about her own daughter's age. It was a dizzying experience, suddenly to hug one's fully grown child. I then embraced my new son and he handed me my tiny granddaughter, whom I did not let go of for the entire visit. I don't think a man was ever happier to hold a baby than I was that day.

Before either Winnie or I knew it, we were in the same room and in each other's arms. I kissed and held my wife for the first time in twenty-one years. It was a moment I had dreamed about a thousand times. It was as if I were still dreaming. I held her to me for what seemed like an eternity. We were still and silent except for the sounds of our hearts. I did not want to let go of her at all.

10 June 1980   After 16 June 1976
Call to the people, published by the ANC abroad.

The rattle of gunfire and the rumbling of Hippo armoured vehicles since June 1976 have once again torn aside the veil of apartheid's constitutional formulas, deceptive phrases and playing with words. Spread across the face of our country, in black townships, the racist army and police have been pouring a hail of bullets, killing and maiming hundreds of black men, women and children.

In the midst of the present crisis, while our people count the dead and nurse the injured, they ask themselves: what lies ahead?

From our rulers we can expect nothing. For they are neither capable nor willing to heed the verdict of the masses of our people.

That verdict is loud and clear: apartheid has failed. Our people remain unequivocal in its rejection. The young and the old, parent and child, all reject it. At the forefront of this 1976/77 wave of unrest were our students and youth. They came trom the universities, high schools and even primary schools. After more than twenty years of Bantu Education the circle is closed and nothing demonstrates the utter bankruptcy of apartheid as does the revolt of our youth.

Our march to freedom is long and difficult. We face an enemy that is deeprooted, an enemy entrenched and determined not to yield. But both within and beyond our borders the prospects of victory grow bright.

The revulsion of the world against apartheid is growing and the frontiers of white supremacy are shrinking. Mozambique and Angola are free and the war of liberation gathers force in Namibia and Zimbabwe. The soil of our country is destined to be the scene of the fiercest fight and the sharpest battles to rid our continent of the last vestiges of white minority rule.

The world is on our side. The OAU, the UN and the anti-apartheid movement continue to put pressure on the racist rulers of our country. Every effort to isolate South Africa adds strength to our struggle.

At all levels of our struggle, within and outside the country, much has been achieved and much remains to be done. But victory is certain!

We who are confined within the grey walls of the Pretoria regime's prisons reach out to our people. With you we count those who have perished by means of the gun and the hangman's rope. We salute all of you – the living, the injured and the dead. For you have dared to rise up against the tyrant's might.

We face the future with confidence. For the guns that serve apartheid cannot render it unconquerable. Those who live by the gun shall perish by the gun.

Between the anvil of united mass action and the hammer of the armed struggle we shall crush apartheid and white minority racist rule.

AMANDLA NGAWETHU!
MATLA KE A RONA!

1 March 1981 *The Prisoner and the Princess*
Letter to Winnie Madikizela Mandela

I hope you will work together with Zindzi, Ismail [Ayob] and George [Bizos] in drafting a letter to those who kindly sponsored our candidature for the Chancellorship of the University of London. To you the support of 7,199 must have been inspiring, turning that miserable shack into a castle, making its narrow rooms as spacious as those of

Windsor. I want all our supporters to know I did not expect to poll even 100, to say nothing of 7,199, against a British princess [Princess Anne, who was elected] and against so distinguished an English reformer as Mr Jack Jones.

4 February 1985   *Your Love and Support*
Letter to Winnie Madikizela Mandela, after hearing of the death of her sister.

Zindzi's telegram reporting the death of Niki shook me violently and I have not recovered yet from the shock. On occasions like this I often wonder just how far more difficult it would have been for me to take the decision to leave you behind if I had been able to see clearly the countless perils and hardships to which you would be exposed in my absence. I sincerely think that my decision would, nonetheless, have been easily the same, but it would certainly have been preceded by far more heart-searching and hesitation than was the case twenty-four years ago.

As I see it, the true significance of marriage lies not only in the mutual love which unites the parties concerned, although that is undoubtedly one of its cornerstones, but also in the faithful support which the parties guarantee – that it will always be there in full measure at critical moments.

Your love and support, the raw warmth of your body, the charming children you have given the family, the many friends you have won, the hope of enjoying that love and warmth again, is what life and happiness mean to me. I have someone I love who is worthy to be loved and trusted, one whose own love and patient support have given me so much strength and hope.

Yet there have been moments when that love and happiness, that trust and hope, have turned into pure agony, when conscience and a sense of guilt have ravaged every part of my being, when I have wondered whether any kind of commitment can ever be sufficient excuse for abandoning a young and inexperienced woman in a pitiless desert, literally throwing her into the hands of highwaymen; a wonderful woman without her pillar and support at times of need.

Knowing full well just how you care for all people, especially the family, I am always extremely worried how you will react to each tragedy. This is what has worried me since Zindzi's telegram arrived, and that concern will not ease until I see you.

10 February 1985 Prisoners Cannot Enter into Contracts

Nelson Mandela's rejection of P W Botha's offer of release on condition he renounce violence was delivered by his daughter Zindzi at Jabulani Stadium, Soweto.

I cherish my own freedom dearly, but I care even more for your freedom. Too many have died since I went to prison. Too many have suffered for the love of freedom. I owe it to their widows, to their orphans, to their mothers and to their fathers who have grieved and wept for them. Not only I have suffered during these long, lonely, wasted years. I am not less life-loving than you are. But I cannot sell my birthright, nor am I prepared to sell the birthright of the people, to be free. I am in prison as the representative of the people and of your organisation, the African National Congress, which was banned.

What freedom am I being offered while the organisation of the people remains banned? What freedom am I being offered when I may be arrested on a pass offence? What freedom am I being offered to live my life as a family with my dear wife who remains in banishment in Brandfort? What freedom am I being offered when I must ask for permission to live in an urban area? What freedom am I being offered when I need a stamp in my pass to seek work? What freedom am I being offered when my very South African citizenship is not respected?

Only free men can negotiate. Prisoners cannot enter into contracts.

I cannot and will not give any undertaking at a time when I and you, the people, are not free.

Your freedom and mine cannot be separated. I will return.

February 1986   The Prisoner's New Clothes
Autobiography

'Mandela,' the commander said, 'we want you to see these people on an equal footing. We don't want you to wear those old prison clothes, so this tailor will take your measurements and outfit you with a proper suit.' The tailor must have been some kind of wizard, for the very next day I tried on a pinstriped suit that fitted me like a glove. The commander admired my new attire: 'Mandela, you look like a prime minister now, not a prisoner.'

24 December 1986   Taken for a Ride
Autobiography

'Mandela, would you like to see the city?'

It was absolutely riveting to watch the simple activities of people out in the world: old men sitting in the sun, women doing their shopping, people walking their dogs. It is precisely those mundane activities of daily life that one misses most in prison.

After an hour or so, Colonel Marx stopped the car in front of a small shop in a quiet street. 'Would you like a cold drink?' he asked. I nodded, and he disappeared inside the shop. For the first few moments I did not think about my situation, but as the seconds ticked away, I became more and more agitated. For the first time in twenty-two years, I was out in the world and unguarded. I had a vision of opening the door, jumping out, and then running and running until I was out of sight. Something inside me was urging me to do just that. I noticed a wooded area near the road where I could hide. I was extremely tense and began to perspire. Where was the colonel? But then I took control of myself; such an action would be unwise and irresponsible, not to mention dangerous. I was greatly relieved when I saw the colonel walking back to the car with two cans of Coca-Cola.

December 1988   Against Doctor's Orders
Autobiography

The breakfast tray contained scrambled eggs, three rashers of bacon and several pieces of buttered toast. I could not remember the last time I had tasted bacon and eggs and I was ravenous. Just as I was about to take a delicious forkful of egg, Major Marais said, 'No, Mandela, that is against the orders of your physician,' and he reached over to take the tray. I held it tightly, and said, 'Major, I am sorry. If this breakfast will kill me, then today I am prepared to die.'

July 1989   Tied up in Knots
Autobiography

Major Marais came into the lounge where I stood in front of him in my suit for inspection. He walked around me and then shook his head from side to side.

'No, Mandela, your tie,' he said. I realised that morning when I was putting it on that I had forgotten how to tie it properly. I made a knot as best I could and hoped that no one would notice. Major Marais, standing behind me, tied it in a double Windsor knot. He then stood back to admire his handiwork. 'Much better,' he said.

We drove to Tuynhuys, the official presidential office. There we were met by Kobie Coetsee, Niel Barnard and a retinue of prison officials. While we were waiting, Dr Barnard looked down and noticed that my shoelaces were not properly tied and he quickly knelt down to tie them for me. I realised just how nervous they were, and that did not make me any calmer. The door then opened and I walked in expecting the worst.

5 July 1989   *No Self-respecting Freedom Fighter*
Document prepared before Nelson Mandela's meeting with P W Botha.

At the outset I must point out that I make this move without consultation with the ANC.

I must stress that no prisoner, irrespective of his status or influence, can conduct negotiations of this nature from prison.

The step I am taking should, therefore, not be seen as the beginning of actual negotiations between the government and the ANC. My task is a very limited one, and that is to bring the country's two major political bodies to the negotiating table. I must further point out that the question of my release from prison is not an issue, at least at this stage of discussions and I am certainly not asking to be freed.

I must emphasise right at this stage that this step is not a response to the call by the government on ANC leaders to declare whether or not they are nationalists and to renounce the South African Communist Party before there can be negotiations: no self-respecting freedom fighter will take orders from the government on how to wage the freedom struggle against that same government and on who his allies in the freedom struggle should be.

The position of the ANC on the question of violence is very simple. The organisation has no vested interest in violence. It abhors any action which may cause loss of life, destruction of property and misery to the people. But we consider the armed struggle a legitimate form of self-defence against a morally repugnant system of government which will not allow even peaceful forms of protest.

White South Africans must accept the plain fact that the ANC will not suspend, to say nothing of abandoning, the armed struggle until the government shows its willingness to surrender the monopoly of political power, and to negotiate directly and in good faith with the acknowledged black leaders. The position of the ANC on the question of violence is, therefore, very clear. A government which used violence against blacks many years before we took up arms has no right whatsoever to call on us to lay down arms.

No worthy leaders of a freedom movement will ever submit to conditions which are essentially terms of surrender dictated by a victorious commander to a beaten enemy, and which are really intended to weaken the organisation or to humiliate its leadership.

The key to the whole situation is a negotiated settlement, and a meeting between the government and the ANC will be the first major step towards lasting peace in the country, better relations with our neighbour states, admission to the Organisation of African Unity, re-admission to the United Nations and other world bodies, to international markets and improved international relations generally.

Lastly, I must point out that the move I have taken provides you with the opportunity to overcome the current deadlock, and to normalise the country's political situation. I hope you will seize it without delay. I believe that the overwhelming majority of South Africans, black and white, hope to see the ANC and the government working closely together to lay the foundations for a new era in our country, in which racial discrimination and prejudice, coercion and confrontation, death and destruction will be forgotten.

12 December 1989   An Honest Commitment to Peace
Document forwarded to F W de Klerk

Mr President,

I hope that Ministers Kobie Coetsee and Gerrit Viljoen have informed you that I deeply appreciate your decision in terms of which eight fellow-prisoners were freed on 15 October 1989, and for advising me of the fact in advance. The release was clearly a major development which rightly evoked praise here and abroad.

In my view it has now become urgent to take other measures to end the present deadlock, and this will certainly be achieved if the government first creates a proper climate for negotiation, followed by a meeting with the ANC. The conflict which is presently draining South Africa's lifeblood either in the form of peaceful demonstrations, acts of violence or external pressure, will never be settled until there is an agreement with the ANC. To this end I have spent more than three years urging the Government to negotiate with the ANC. I hope I will not leave this place with empty hands

The Government insists on the ANC making an honest commitment to peace before it will talk to the organisation. It must be made clear at the outset that the ANC will never make such a commitment at the instance of the Government, or any other source for that matter. We would have thought that the history of this country's liberation movement, especially during the last 41 years, would have made that point perfectly clear.

The whole approach of the Government to the question of negotiation with the ANC is totally unacceptable, and requires to be drastically changed. No serious political organisation will ever talk peace when an aggressive war is being waged against it. No proud people will ever obey orders from those who have humiliated and dishonoured them for so long.

The Government ought to be aware that readiness to negotiate is in itself an honest commitment to peace. In this regard, the ANC is far ahead of the Government. It has repeatedly declared its willingness to negotiate, provided a proper climate for such negotiations exists.

There is neither logic nor common sense in asking the ANC to do now what it has consistently done on countless occasions before. It is the Government, not the ANC, that started civil war in this country, and that does not want reconciliation and peace. How can one work for reconciliation and peace under a State of Emergency, with black areas under military occupation, when people's organisations are banned, leaders are either in exile, prison or restricted, when the policy of apartheid with its violence is still being enforced, and when no conditions for free political expression exist?

I should like to believe that my exploratory efforts during the last three years have not been in vain, that I have an important role still to play in helping to bring about a peaceful settlement, that the initiatives you have already taken will soon be followed by other developments on the really fundamental issues that are agitating our people, and that in our lifetime our country will rid itself of the pestilence of racialism in all its forms.

STATESMAN

11 February 1990   Meeting the People
Autobiography

When the crowd had started to settle down, I took out my speech and then reached into my breast pocket for my glasses. They were not there; I had left them at Victor Verster. I knew Winnie's glasses had a similar prescription, and I borrowed hers.

11 February 1990   I Stand Here Before You
Speech following release, City Hall, Cape Town

Friends, comrades, and fellow South Africans,

I greet you all in the name of peace, democracy, and freedom for all. I stand here before you not as a prophet but as a humble servant of you, the people. Your tireless and heroic sacrifices have made it possible for me to be here today. I therefore place the remaining years of my life in your hands.

On this day of my release, I extend my sincere and warmest gratitude to the millions of my compatriots and those in every corner of the globe who have campaigned tirelessly for my release.

Today the majority of South Africans, black and white, recognise that apartheid has no future. It has to be ended by our own decisive mass action in order to build peace and security. The mass campaigns of defiance and other actions of our organisation and people can only culminate in the establishment of democracy.

The apartheid destruction on our subcontinent is incalculable. The family life of millions of my people has been shattered. Millions are homeless and unemployed. Our economy lies in ruins and our people are embroiled in political strife.

The need to unite the people of our country is as important a task now as it always has been. No individual leader is able to take on this enormous task on his own. It is our task as leaders to place our views before our organisation and to allow the democratic structures to decide on the way forward.

Our struggle has reached a decisive moment. We call on our people to seize this moment so that the process towards democracy is rapid and uninterrupted. We have waited too long for our freedom. We can no longer wait. Now is the time to intensify the struggle on all fronts.

To relax our efforts now would be a mistake which generations to come will not be able to forgive. The sight of freedom looming on the horizon should encourage us to redouble our efforts. It is only through disciplined mass action that our victory can be assured.

Our march to freedom is irreversible. We must not allow fear to stand in our way.

Universal suffrage on a common voters' roll in a united, democratic, and non-racial South Africa is the only way to peace and racial harmony.

In conclusion, I wish to go to my own words during my

trial in 1964. They are as true today as they were then. I quote: 'During my lifetime I have dedicated myself to this struggle of the African people. I have fought against white domination, and I have fought against black domination. I have cherished the ideal of a democratic and free society in which all persons live together in harmony and with equal opportunities. It is an ideal which I hope to live for and to achieve. But if needs be, it is an ideal for which I am prepared to die.'

13 February 1990   Return to School and Learn
Address at welcome rally in Soweto

Today, my return to Soweto fills my heart with joy. At the same time I also return with a deep sense of sadness. Sadness to learn that you are still suffering under an inhuman system. The housing shortage, the schools crisis, unemployment and the crime rate still remain.

I am even more proud to be a member of this community because of the pioneering role it has played in the struggle for the democratisation of local government. You have built democratic structures of local government in Soweto such as street committees and civic organisations that give practical import to our desire to let the people govern.

As proud as I am to be part of the Soweto community, I have been greatly disturbed by the statistics of crime that I have read in the newspapers. Although I understand the deprivations our people suffer, I must make it clear that the level of crime in our township is unhealthy and must be eliminated as a matter of urgency.

The crisis in education that exists in South Africa demands special attention. I want to add my voice to the call made at the beginning of the year that all students must return to school and learn. We have consistently called for a unitary non-racial education system that develops the potential of all our youth.

Our struggle against apartheid, though seemingly uncertain, must be intensified on all fronts. Let each one of you and all of our people give the enemies of peace and liberty no space to take us back to the dark hell of apartheid.

Go back to your schools, factories, mines and communities. Build on the massive energies that recent events in our country have unleashed by strengthening disciplined mass organisations.

We are going forward. The march towards freedom and justice is irreversible. I have spoken about freedom in my lifetime. Your struggles, your commitment and your discipline have released me to stand here before you today. These basic principles will propel us to a free, non-racial, democratic, united South Africa that we have struggled and died for.

25 February 1990   End This War Now!
Address at welcome rally in Durban

Friends, comrades, and the people of Natal, I greet you all. I do so in the name of peace, the peace that is so desperately and urgently needed in this region.

In Natal, apartheid is a deadly cancer in our midst, setting house against house, and eating away at the precious ties that bound us together. My message to those of you involved in this battle of brother against brother is this: take your guns, your knives, and your pangas, and throw them into the sea. Close down the death factories. End this war now!

It is vital that we end the conflict in Natal, and end it now. Everyone must commit themselves to peace. Women of Natal, in the past and at crucial moments, you have shown greater wisdom than your menfolk. Mothers, sisters and daughters of Natal, it falls to you once again to intervene decisively. Tell your sons, your brothers, and your husbands that you want peace and security. Open the cooking pots and ask the men why there is so little food inside. When the rains come into your homes, place the hands of your men in the pools on the floor, and ask them, why? When your child ails, and you have no money to take it to the doctor, ask them, why? Go out and meet the women on the other side. Their story is the same. Then take your men with you. We place our trust in you.

Since my release, I have become more convinced than ever that the real makers of history are the ordinary men and women of our country. It is only the united action of you, the people, that will ensure that freedom is finally achieved. Together we shall conquer!

November 1990   We Salute the Mothers
Speech to ANC Workshop on Gender Issues

Throughout the history of our struggle, women have played a prominent role. To mention but a few: our stalwarts such as Charlotte Maxeke, Dora Tamana, Ruth First, Annie Silinga, Mary Moodley, Lilian Ngoyi, Kate Molale, and Florence Mophosho. Their fighting spirit lives on in the contribution of such eminent women as Mrs M Zihlangu, Frances Baard, Helen Joseph, Ray Simons, Dorothy Nyembe, Gertrude Shope, and many others.

We salute the mothers of the cadres of Umkhonto weSizwe, whose children have fallen in battle both inside and outside South Africa. We pay tribute to the mothers of all those who died in the course of the struggle for freedom and against the apartheid system. We commend also those white mothers who stood by their sons for refusing to be conscripted into the apartheid army. We salute the wives and mothers whose husbands and sons still remain in prison despite the solemn undertakings of the apartheid regime. We salute those brave daughters of this country who are presently in prison for their commitment to a just, non-racial, and democratic South Africa.

The South African society is profoundly patriarchal. While ultimate responsibility falls squarely on the shoulders of the ruling circles of this country, we men, both black and white, including many in the ANC, should accept our share of responsibility for the sexist stereotyping of women in our society and in our homes.

Women in South Africa constitute the majority population; yet, in general, their status is one of powerlessness. They are under-represented in all sectors of our society, except its lower reaches. This, unfortunately, also applies to the leadership of the ANC and all democratic organisations of this country.

For decades institutionalised racism has been applied by the apartheid state to effect the most brutal forms of social engineering known to humanity. Need I remind this workshop that millions of black women remain illiterate in the age of advanced education and technology? That black women, in thousands, occupy the lowest ranks in employment? That black women are underpaid and are most brutally exploited as farm labourers and domestic workers? For generations, black women have been the most oppressed group in our society.

I would like to put forward, for your consideration, the proposal that the constitution for a new South Africa should unequivocally state that South Africa should not only be unitary, non-racial, and democratic, but should also be a non-sexist state.

20 December 1991   Like a Schoolmaster
Autobiography

He began to speak to us like a schoolmaster admonishing a naughty child. This was more than I could tolerate and I would now be damned if I would permit Mr de Klerk to have the last word. When he finished, the meeting was meant to be over. But the room had grown very quiet; instead of allowing the session to end, I walked to the podium. I could not let his remarks go unchallenged. My voice betrayed my anger.

20 December 1991   Less Than Frank
Impromptu Speech in reply to F W de Klerk at the end of the first day of the Codesa meetings

I am gravely concerned about the behaviour of Mr de Klerk today. He has launched an attack on the ANC and in doing so he has been less than frank. Even the head of an illegitimate, discredited minority regime, as his is, has certain moral standards to uphold. It is no wonder the Conservative Party has made such serious inroads into his power base. You can understand why. If a man can come to a conference of this nature and play the type of politics as is in his paper – very few people would like to deal with such a man.

We have had bilateral discussons, but although I was discussing with him until about twenty minutes past eight last night, he never even hinted that he was going to make this attack.

The members of the government persuaded us to allow them to speak last. They were very keen to say the last word here. It is now clear why they did so. He has abused his position, because he hoped that I would not respond. He was completely mistaken. I respond now.

I say he is less than frank, because he has not told you that it is the African National Congress, not the National

Party, nor P W [Botha], that started this initiative. I have been discussing with top government officials since July 1986 when I was still in prison, asking that the ANC and the government sit down to explore a peaceful solution.

As a result of the pressure of the people inside the country and of the international community, and as a result of persuasion from us, they eventually agreed to sit down to discuss with us. We have gone along with the creation of an atmosphere whereby these negotiations can succeed. As part of that process we suspended the armed struggle.

What has been happening on the side of the government? We suspended the armed struggle in spite of the fact that our people were being killed. And the government – with all its capacity to put an end to violence – was doing nothing to stop the slaughter of innocent people.

Now he is attacking us because we have not dissolved MK. We had discussions in Cape Town and Pretoria on Umkhonto weSizwe. We had an agreement in terms of which we had to hand over our weapons for joint control by the government and ourselves.

I regret very much that he should try to take advantage of this meeting for petty political gains. It concerns what we have been saying all along: that the National Party and the government have a double agenda.

They are talking peace while at the same time conducting a war against us.

If Mr de Klerk promises to do his duty as the head of government – to put an end to the violence, to restrain his security services, to clean the country of hit squads killing innocent people – then he can come to us and say, 'I want you to hand over your weapons to us for joint control.' But as long as he is playing this double game he must be clear that we are not going to cooperate with him on this matter. He can do what he wants. We are not going to disband Umkhonto weSizwe.

I ask him to place his cards on the table face upwards. Let's work together openly. Let there be no secret agendas.

I am prepared to make allowances because he is a product of apartheid. Although he wants these democratic changes, he has sometimes very little idea of what democracy means. He is forgetting that he cannot speak like a representative of a government which has both legitimacy and which represents the majority of the population. These are statements that can only be used by somebody who represents the majority of the country. He doesn't represent us. He can't talk to us in that language.

This type of thing, of trying to take advantage of the cooperation which we have given him willingly, is something that is very dangerous and I hope that this is the last time he will do so.

13 April 1992   *The Pain I Have Gone Through*
Statement given at a press conference to announce his separation from his wife Nomzamo Winnie Madikizela Mandela

Comrade Nomzamo and myself contracted our marriage at a critical time in the struggle for liberation in our country. Owing to the pressures of our shared commitment to the

ANC and the struggle to end apartheid we were unable to enjoy a normal family life.

Despite these pressures our love for each other and our devotion to our marriage grew and intensified. Her tenacity reinforced my personal respect, love and growing affection.

During both my trials, the first in 1962 and during the Rivonia trial of 1964, Comrade Nomzamo was the key figure in mobilising solidarity and support for myself and the other Rivonia trialists, alongside other members of the ANC and its allies.

She endured the persecutions heaped upon her by the Government with exemplary fortitude and never wavered from her commitment to the struggle for freedom.

In view of the tensions which have arisen owing to differences between ourselves on a number of issues in recent months, we have mutually agreed that a separation would be best for each of us.

I part from my wife with no recriminations. I embrace her with all the love and affection I have nursed for her inside and outside prison from the moment I first met her.

Ladies and gentlemen, I hope you appreciate the pain I have gone through.

17 June 1992   The Last Straw
Autobiography

The police did nothing. Mr de Klerk said nothing. This was the last straw, and my patience snapped. Why were we continuing to talk with them?

21 June 1992   We Keep Talking Peace
Speech to the residents of Boipatong

I am here to express my deepest sympathies to the people of Boipatong and Slovo Park for one of the most brutal slaughters of human beings in the history of this country. Innocent and defenceless men, women and children – pregnant women and unsuspecting babies – were not exempted from the bullets and spears of the faceless murderers who work closely with the regime and its security services.

Early in 1960, sixty-seven bodies of unarmed men, women and children were strewn over the veld in Sharpeville, with four hundred people injured. I come back to Boipatong, where Sharpeville has been repeated with a ferocity that may completely put an end to negotiations.

Mr de Klerk and his regime bear full responsibility for the violence in the country, and in these townships in particular. According to the press, Mr de Klerk expressed shock and concern over the slaughter. Strange that he should be shocked and now suddenly express concern. Why is he shocked now? While these latest killings are horrific, the reality is that there are a number of massacres that have taken place where deaths turn into double figures.

Heads of state throughout the world express their sympathies to families in cases of disaster. Mr de Klerk has been strangely silent when black deaths are involved. We welcome his sympathy message, but it comes with crocodile tears.

What is our response to this challenge? The negotiation process is clearly in disarray. I am calling an emergency meeting of the National Executive Committee of the ANC to examine options. I can no longer explain to our people why we keep talking peace to men who are conducting a war against us, men of corruption who kill innocent people.

There is a bilateral meeting between the ANC and the National Party scheduled to meet on Tuesday. I have instructed the secretary-general to cancel that meeting.

As far as the international community is concerned, I am going to request the Secretary General of the UN to call a special session of the Security Council on the massacres committed by Mr de Klerk and his regime. I will address that session.

10 April 1993   To Cofimvaba, to Pay My Respects
Autobiography

Chris's eighty-two-year-old father in Sabalele, a tiny dusty town in the Cofimvaba district in the Transkei, spoke eloquently of the pain of losing a son, but with satisfaction that he had died in the struggle. It was the ANC, not the government, that sought to calm the people.

13 April 1993   Honour This Soldier for Peace
Television address to the nation following the assassination of Chris Hani

Tonight I am reaching out to every single South African, black and white, from the very depths of my being.

A white man, full of prejudice and hate, came to our country and committed a deed so foul that our whole nation now teeters on the brink of disaster. A white woman, of Afrikaner origin, risked her life so that we may know, and bring to justice, this assassin.

The cold-blooded murder of Chris Hani has sent shock waves throughout the country and the world. Our grief and anger is tearing us apart. What has happened is a national tragedy that has touched millions of people, across the political and colour divide.

Now is the time for all South Africans to stand together against those who, from any quarter, wish to destroy what Chris Hani gave his life for: the freedom of all of us.

This is a watershed moment for all of us. Our decisions and actions will determine whether we use our pain, our grief, and our outrage to move forward to what is the only lasting solution for our country: an elected government of the people, by the people, and for the people.

We must not let the men who worship war, and who lust after blood, precipitate actions that will plunge our country into another Angola.

Chris Hani was a soldier. He believed in iron discipline. He carried out instructions to the letter. He practised what he preached.

Let us honour this soldier for peace in a fitting manner. Let us rededicate ourselves to bringing about the democracy he fought for all his life; democracy that will bring real, tangible changes in the lives of the working people, the poor, the jobless, the landless.

To the youth of South Africa we have a special message. You have lost a great hero. You have repeatedly shown that your love of freedom is greater than that most precious gift, life itself. But you are the leaders of tomorrow. Your country, your people, your organisation need you to act with wisdom. A particular responsibility rests on your shoulders.

Chris Hani made the supreme sacrifice. The greatest tribute we can pay to his life's work is to ensure we win that freedom for all our people.

27 April 1993   *A Life-long Conversation*
Autobiography

Adelaide phoned me early in the morning and I rushed to Oliver's bedside. I did not have a chance to say a proper good-bye, for he was already gone. Though we had been apart for all the years that I was in prison, Oliver was never far from my thoughts. In many ways, even though we were separated, I kept up a life-long conversation with him in my head. Perhaps that is why I felt so bereft when he died. I felt like the loneliest man in the world.

14 June 1993   A Job to Do
Interview with 'Time' magazine

TIME: Three and a half years ago, you were still under arrest. Now you're engaged in the process of rebuilding the country. Did you ever think this was going to happen in your lifetime?

MANDELA: There were definitely moments when I was not so certain that day would come. But, as you know, I did send a message that was read by my daughter at a public meeting where I said, 'I will return.' So that perception was always there. But that doesn't mean there weren't moments when I doubted whether this moment would come. But the strength of the struggle in the country and the support of the international community has always been powerful, and that kept our morale very high, and it made us feel that the forces of change were too powerful to be ignored by the government.

TIME: Many have commented about your lack of bitterness. How could you put the past behind you?

MANDELA: Perhaps if I was idle and did not have a job to do, I would be as bitter as others. But because I have been given a job to do, I have not had time to think about the cruel experiences I've had. I'm not unique. Others have every reason to be more bitter than I. There are countless people who went to jail and aren't bitter at all, because they can see that their sacrifices were not in vain, and the ideas for which we lived and sacrificed are about to come to fruition. And that removes the bitterness from their hearts.

2 May 1994   What the Doctor Ordered
Autobiography

I was suffering from a bad case of flu and my doctors ordered me to remain at home. But nothing could keep me away from that victory party at the Carlton Hotel. I went on stage at about nine o'clock and faced a crowd of happy, smiling, cheering faces. I explained that my voice was hoarse from a cold and that my physician had advised me not to attend: 'I hope that you will not disclose to him that I have violated his instructions.'

2 May 1994   Free at Last
Victory Speech after the results of the first democratic elections

My fellow South Africans – the people of South Africa,

This is indeed a joyous night for the human spirit. This is your victory. You helped end apartheid, you stood with us through the transition.

I watched, along with all of you, as tens of thousands of our people stood patiently in long queues for many hours, some sleeping on the open veld overnight, waiting to cast this momentous vote.

South Africa's heroes are legend across the generations, but it is you, the people, who are our true heroes.

This is one of the most important moments in the life of our country. I stand here before you filled with a deep pride and joy. Pride in the ordinary humble people of this country: you have shown such a calm patient determination to reclaim this country as your own. And joy that we can loudly proclaim from the rooftops: free at last!

I stand before you humbled by your courage, with a heart full of love for all of you. I regard it as the highest honour to lead the African National Congress at this moment in our history, and that we have been chosen to lead our country into a new century.

Tomorrow the entire ANC leadership and I will be back at our desks. We are rolling up our sleeves to begin tackling the problems our country faces. We ask you all to join us. Go back to your jobs in the morning. Let's get South Africa working.

Now is the time for celebration, for South Africans to join together to celebrate the birth of democracy. I raise a glass to you all for working so hard to achieve what can only be called a small miracle.

I promise that I will do my best to be worthy of the faith and confidence you have placed in me and my organisation, the ANC.

Let us build the future together, and toast a better life for all South Africans.

PRESIDENT

10 May 1994   The Day Dawned
Autobiography

10 May dawned bright and clear. On that lovely autumn day I was accompanied by my daughter Zenani.

10 May 1994 I Do Hereby Swear
Inauguration: the Presidential Oath of Office

In the presence of those assembled here and in full realisation of the high calling I assume as the executive President in the service of the Republic of South Africa, I, Nelson Rolihlahla Mandela, do hereby swear to be faithful to the Republic of South Africa, and do solemnly and sincerely promise at all times to promote that which will advance and to oppose that which may harm the Republic, to obey, observe, uphold and maintain the Constitution and all other laws of the Republic, to discharge my duties with all my strength and talents to the best of my knowledge and ability, and, true to the dictates of my conscience, to do justice to all, and to devote myself to the well-being of the Republic and all its people. So help me, God.

10 May 1994   Never, Never and Never Again
Presidential Address at the Inauguration

Today, all of us do, by our presence here, and by our cele-
brations in other parts of the country and the world, confer
glory and hope to new-born liberty.

Out of the experience of an extraordinary human disaster that lasted too long must be born a society of which all
humanity will be proud.

Our daily deeds as ordinary South Africans must produce an actual South African reality that will reinforce
humanity's belief in justice, strengthen its confidence in the
nobility of the human soul and sustain all our hopes for a
glorious life for all.

To my compatriots, I have no hesitation in saying that
each one of us is as intimately attached to the soil of this
beautiful country as are the famous jacaranda trees of
Pretoria and the mimosa trees of the bushveld.

Each time one of us touches the soil of this land, we feel
a sense of personal renewal. The national mood changes as
the seasons change.

We are moved by a sense of joy and exhilaration when
the grass turns green and the flowers bloom.

That spiritual and physical oneness we all share with this
common homeland explains the depth of the pain we all
carried in our hearts as we saw our country tear itself apart
in a terrible conflict, and as we saw it spurned, outlawed
and isolated by the people of the world, precisely because
it had become the universal base of the pernicious ideology

and practice of racism and racial oppression.

We, the people of South Africa, feel fulfilled that humanity has taken us back into its bosom, that we, who were outlaws not so long ago, have today been given the rare privilege to be host to the nations of the world on our own soil .

We thank all our distinguished international guests for having come to take possession with the people of our country of what is, after all, a common victory for justice, for peace, for human dignity.

We trust that you will continue to stand by us as we tackle the challenges of building peace, prosperity, non-sexism, non-racialism and democracy.

We deeply appreciate the role that the masses of our people and their political mass democratic, religious, women, youth, business, traditional and other leaders have played to bring about this conclusion. Not least among them is my Second Deputy President, the Honourable F W de Klerk.

The time for the healing of the wounds has come. The moment to bridge the chasms that divide us has come. The time to build is upon us.

We have, at last, achieved our political emancipation. We pledge ourselves to liberate all our people from the continuing bondage of poverty, deprivation, suffering, gender and other discrimination.

We succeeded in taking our last steps to freedom in conditions of relative peace. We commit ourselves to the construction of a complete, just and lasting peace.

We have triumphed in the effort to implant hope in the

breasts of the millions of our people. We enter into a covenant that we shall build the society in which all South Africans, both black and white, will be able to walk tall, without any fear in their hearts, assured of their inalienable right to human dignity – a rainbow nation at peace with itself and the world.

We dedicate this day to all the heroes and heroines in this country and the rest of the world who sacrificed in many ways and surrendered their lives so that we could be free. Their dreams have become reality. Freedom is their reward.

We understand it still that there is no easy road to freedom. We know it well that none of us acting alone can achieve success. We must therefore act together as a united people, for national reconciliation, for nation building, for the birth of a new world.

Let there be justice for all. Let there be peace for all. Let there be work, bread, water and salt for all.

Let each know that, for each, the body, the mind and the soul have been freed to fulfil themselves.

Never, never and never again shall it be that this beautiful land will again experience the oppression of one by another, and suffer the indignity of being the skunk of the world.

The sun shall never set on so glorious a human achievement.

Let freedom reign.

God bless Africa.

10 May 1994   *That Other Force*
Inauguration: Impromptu Speech at the lunch

Many forces have influenced the history of our country, as they have done in the history of other countries. The workers, traditional leaders and tribesmen from the countryside, educationists, economists, businessmen, religious leaders: all have played a role in our history. But just for one or two moments I want to talk about two forces which have been of particular relevance in the history of our country.

We are aware of the type of government we have had since 1910, which relied on brute force and coercion. The many decades of that coercion only served to produce the Mbekis, the Sisulus, the Joe Slovos, the Bram Fischers, the Dadoos, the Naickers, the Trevor Manuels; and they have become national heroes today and some of them are now holding cabinet posts. They prevailed after a lot of bitterness had been created, and it is as a result of that policy that deep wounds have been created in our country: coercion, brute force, impatience, the inability to sit down with your countrymen and to talk.

But there has been another force: that of compassion, that of love and loyalty to your country, that of ignoring what is negative in a human being and concentrating on that which is good. Through dialogue, through persuasion, we have been able to bring South Africa out of the era of darkness, bitterness, pessimism, to a moment where the entire world has joined us to come and celebrate.

That is a lesson, not just for this day; it is a lesson on

which we can build for the future. Perhaps it was fortunate that we had this era, because we are now able to appreciate the sacrifices that have been made by the Sisulus, the Mbekis and the others. We now know the calibre of the men and women of South Africa. South Africa is rich not only in natural wealth and gold; it is rich in the calibre of its men and women. We appreciate that, and we have come to appreciate it more because of the struggle they put forward.

But there is another aspect. From the opposite direction, among those who have been produced by apartheid, there have been men and women with a vision, who realised that human beings are human beings. I spent so many years in prison ... you will be surprised to know the friendships, the strong friendships, that were built between black prisoners and white warders. It was difficult for the policy-makers to persecute us as they wanted, because we became friends with the warders in our prison. It was through them that we could be persecuted, and the firm friendships that we formed were themselves a protection. I don't know whether my friends are here: I invited three of the warders who looked after me to attend this celebration. I invited them to come because I wanted them to share in the joys that have emanated spontaneously around this day, because, in a way, they also contributed to it.

Then, of course, there's my friend, Mr de Klerk. He was one of those who gave us a hard time. The late Dr Danie Craven and Dr Luyt went to Harare to see the ANC. When they came back, they were chastised by Mr de Klerk for having discussions with a terrorist organisation.

I mention this as a measure of the change he has undergone, the personal courage, the vision, the honesty, the integrity with which he came to examine the situation in South Africa, and used his enormous power as the head of the government to bring about reforms.

So, we have forgotten the past. We must know the past, so that, when we work together now in a Government of National Unity, we must know precisely what we have come through, what we should avoid. We have said a lot of unkind things about one another during the election, but we have fought the election, we have had a good fight; now it is time for us to put together the broken pieces of our country and to ensure that our people speak with one voice.

We feel, because of the many years of discussions which we have had – before I was released from jail I had meetings with him, we discussed the situation together – and then during these four years we have exchanged on a wide variety of very sensitive issues. When our own teams could not agree, we sat down together and exchanged views. I took him into my confidence about some of the problems that I had; he took me into his confidence about the problems he had, and we worked as a team behind the scenes, and we were able to keep together at one time 26 political parties, with different backgrounds, pulling in different directions.

Today is the result of that other force in our country, that of persuasion, that of discussing, that of dialogue, that of love and loyalty to our common fatherland. In the days to come this is the force on which we are going to rely. We are still going to have many problems, which the Government of National Unity will have to face. But I have no doubt that we have the men and women in this country, from all sections of the population, who will rise to the challenge.

1994   Discovering the Secret
Autobiography

I have walked that long road to freedom. I have tried not to falter; I have made missteps along the way. But I have discovered the secret that after climbing a great hill, one only finds that there are many more hills to climb. I have taken a moment here to rest, to steal a view of the glorious vista that surrounds me, to look back on the distance I have come. But I can rest only for a moment, for with freedom come responsibilities, and I dare not linger, for my long walk is not yet ended.

24 April 1997   A Very Amazing Experience
Interview with Daphne Barak. The final moments of the interview concerned President Mandela's relationship with Mrs Graca Machel.

BARAK: I must ask you a question that my mother has been asking me and my partner for years. What about marriage?

MANDELA: Oh ... [*he laughs, embarrassed*] my dear young lady, I am very lucky. When will I marry? I don't exactly know.

BARAK: But what a wonderful happy ending to your story of years in prison, self-sacrifice, a split-up family, and here you are, a president, and in love.

MANDELA: To be in love is an experience that every man must go through. For me, it's a very amazing experience. One should be so grateful at being involved in such an experience. It is such a wonderful period for me.

Grateful acknowledgements are due for permission to quote the material in this book, all of which emanates from Nelson Mandela and is copyrighted in his name.

Autobiography

A Long Walk to Freedom (Little, Brown and Company, Inc., Boston, 1994)

Letters, articles and speeches

Thomas Karis and Gwendolen M Carter (eds.): *From Protest to Challenge: A Documentary History of African Politics in South Africa 1882–1964*. Volume 3: *Challenge and Violence 1953–64* ed. by Thomas Karis and Gail M Gerhart (Hoover Institution Press, Stanford, 1977)

Nelson Mandela: *The Struggle Is My Life* (IDAF Publications, London, 1990; Mayibuye Books, University of the Western Cape, in association with David Philip, Cape Town, 1994)

Nelson Mandela: *Nelson Mandela Speaks: Forging a Democratic Nonracial South Africa* (David Philip, Cape Town, in association with Mayibuye Books, University of the Western Cape, 1994)

Winnie Mandela, edited by Anne Benjamin, adapted by Mary Benson: *Part of My Soul* (Penguin, Harmondsworth, 1985)

Emma Gilbey: *The Lady: The Life and Times of Winnie Mandela* (Vintage, London, 1994)